Bob Chilcott

Jazz Folk Songs for Choirs

9 songs from around the world

for mixed voices and jazz trio or piano solo

MUSIC DEPARTMENT

OXFORD
UNIVERSITY PRESS

OXFORD
UNIVERSITY PRESS

Great Clarendon Street, Oxford OX2 6DP, England
198 Madison Avenue, New York, NY 10016, USA

Oxford University Press is a department of the University of Oxford.
It furthers the University's aim of excellence in research, scholarship,
and education by publishing worldwide

Oxford is a registered trade mark of Oxford University Press
in the UK and in certain other countries

© Oxford University Press 2008

Bob Chilcott has asserted his right under the Copyright, Designs
and Patents Act, 1988, to be identified as the Arranger of these Works

Database right Oxford University Press (maker)

First published 2008

All rights reserved. No part of this publication may be reproduced,
stored in a retrieval system, or transmitted, in any form or by any means,
without the prior permission in writing of Oxford University Press,
or as expressly permitted by law. Enquiries concerning reproduction
outside the scope of the above should be sent to the Music Copyright
Department, Oxford University Press, at the address above

Permission to perform the works in this anthology in public
(except in the course of divine worship) should normally be obtained
from the Performing Right Society Ltd. (PRS), 29/33 Berners Street,
London W1T 3AB, or its affiliated Societies in each country throughout
the world, unless the owner or the occupier of the premises
being used holds a licence from the Society

Permission to make a recording must be obtained in advance
from the Mechanical-Copyright Protection Society Ltd. (MCPS),
Elgar House, 41 Streatham High Road, London SW16 1ER,
or its affiliated Societies in each country throughout the world

11

ISBN 978-0-19-335924-6 (main edition)
ISBN 978-0-19-336182-9 (spiral-bound with CD)

Music origination by Enigma Music Production Services, Amersham, Bucks.
Printed in Great Britain on acid-free paper by
Halstan & Co. Ltd., Amersham, Bucks.

Contents

Composer's note v

À la claire fontaine (There by the crystal fountain) 2

En la Macarenita (Down in the Macarena) 9

Hush, little baby 25

Sakura (Cherry tree) 32

Scarborough Fair 36

Tell my ma 43

The House of the Rising Sun 52

Tuoll' on mun kultani (There is my loved one) 59

Waltzing Matilda 66

CD track list and credits 80

Composer's note

When I was a choir and ensemble singer I always loved to perform pieces influenced by jazz. The style creates a real sense of energy and presents an interesting choral challenge in terms of blend, intonation, rhythm, phrasing, and making often well-known songs sound natural and true. In this book I have taken nine folk-song tunes and tried to create a palette of different jazz-influenced styles and colours that I hope choirs will enjoy working at. The songs can be performed by choir and piano, or by choir and jazz trio (piano, bass, and drums), and other instruments could also be added to the ensemble. The piano parts work well as notated in the book, but many players might like to improvise and solo, which would be fine too.

Structurally, most of the songs work best if performed as written. However, there is the opportunity in both 'Tuoll' on mun kultani' and 'Waltzing Matilda' to include a repeated section for solo instrumentalists or scat singers; instructions are written in the score. The Andalusian song 'En la Macarenita' was written for the inspirational Cuban vocal group Novel Voz, which is lucky enough to have within its ranks a singer who is wonderful at beatboxing, or vocal percussion. These kinds of effects would work really well in this song, should a member of the choir be willing to give them a go!

I would like to thank the editors Robyn Carpenter and Mary Chandler for their work on this volume, and also the pianist Alex Hawkins for his annotation of the bass parts and for playing on the backing CD (included with the spiral-bound edition) with Michael Chilcott and Derek Scurll.

Bob Chilcott, June 2008

for Jon Washburn and the Vancouver Chamber Choir

À la claire fontaine

(There by the crystal fountain)

English version BC

Trad. French Canadian
arr. BOB CHILCOTT

© Oxford University Press 2008. Photocopying this copyright material is ILLEGAL.

9
11
A.
Sous les feuil - les d'un chê - ne je me suis fait sé - cher,
And as I lay to shel - ter un - der a sha - dy tree,
mp dolce espress.
T.
Sous les feuil - les d'un chê - ne je me suis fait sé -
And as I lay to shel - ter un - der a sha - dy
13
Sur la plus hau - te bran - che, un ros - si - gnol chan - tait.
I heard a night - in - gale who sang out his song to me.
- cher, le ros - si - gnol chan - tait.
tree, he sang his song to me.

15
mf
S.
A.
ja - mais je ne t'ou - blie - rai.
Time can't stop me lov - ing you.
ja - mais je ne t'ou - blie - rai.
Time can't stop me lov - ing you.
Il y a long-temps que je t'ai-me,
How can I be - gin to for-get you?
T.
B.
mf
ja - mais je ne t'ou - blie - rai.
Time can't stop me lov - ing you.
mf
19
f
S.
A.
oo
f
T.
oo
f
B.
Chan - te, ros - si-gnol, chan - te, toi qui as le cœur gai, Tu as le cœur à ri - re
Sing out your song so ten - der, sing out your song a - gain, Your heart feels so en-chant-ed,
3
3
3
3
f

22
Il y a long-temps que je t'ai - me,
How can I be - gin to for - get you?
Il y a long-temps que je t'ai - me,
How can I be - gin to for - get you?
moi je l'ai à pleu - rer.
mine feels con - sumed with pain.
Il y a long-temps que je t'ai - me,
How can I be - gin to for - get you?
24
mf
oo
mf
oo
mf
ja - mais je ne t'ou-blie-rai.
Time can't stop me lov - ing you.
mf

27
mp
S.
J'ai per - du mon a - mi - e sans l'a - voir mé - ri - té,
I lost my on - ly lov - er and still I don't know why,
mp
T.
J'ai per - du mon a - mi - e sans l'a - voir mé - ri -
I lost my lov - er and still I don't know
mp
29
pour un bou - quet de ro - ses que je lui re - fu - sais.
All for a bunch of ro - ses; that I can - not de - ny.
- té, pour un bou - quet de ro - ses, de ro - ses.
why, for a bunch of ro - ses, of ro - ses.
31
S.
Il y a long - temps que je t'ai - me, ja - mais je ne t'ou - blie - rai,
How can I be - gin to for - get you? Time can't stop me lov - ing you.
div.
mp
A.
oo
T.
B.
oo

33
je ne t'ou-blie - rai.
stop me lov - ing you.
p espress.
36
A.
unis.
p espress.
Je vou drais que la ro - se fût en-core au ro - sier,
I wish the bunch of ro - ses still grew for all to see,
39
Et que ma douce a - mi - e fût en - core à m'ai - mer.
And that my gen - tle lov - er still lived for lov - ing me.

41
S.
A.
T.
B.
p
oo
Il y a long-temps que je t'ai - me, ja - mais je ne t'ou - blie - rai.
How can I be - gin to for - get you? Time can't stop me lov - ing you.
43
3
div.
rit.
pp

for Novel Voz

En la Macarenita
(Down in the Macarena)

English version BC

Trad. Andalusian
arr. BOB CHILCOTT

Cool, with a samba feel ♩ = c.152
SOPRANO
ALTO
TENOR
BASS
mp
la la la

8
en la Ma-ca-re-ni-ta me die-ron
down in the Ma-ca-re-na, I caught his
la la la la la la la la la la la la la
la la la la la la la la la la la la la
dm d d dm dm dm d dm dm
11
a-gua más frí-a que la nie-ve en u-na
glan-ces. I like the way he woos me, the way he
la la la la la la la la la la la la la la la la la la la la
la la la la la la la la la la la la la la la la la la la la
dm dm dm d d dm dm dm dm dm dm

15
S.
(mf)
ta - ya.
danc - es.
la la la la la la la la la la la la la la la
A.
mf
unis.
ta - ya. La Ma-ca - re - na. Bue-na ca - pa; buen som - bre - ro; bue-na
danc - es. The Ma-ca - re - na. Got a good coat; got a good hat; it's a
T.
mf
ta - ya.
danc - es.
la la la la la la la la la la la la la la la
T. 1
mf
ta - ya. La Ma-ca - re - na. Bue-na ca - pa; buen som - bre - ro; bue-na
danc - es. The Ma-ca - re - na. Got a good coat; got a good hat; it's a
T. 2
mf
ta - ya.
danc - es.
dm dm dm dm d dm dm dm dm d dm
mf
19
la la la la la la la la la la la la la la la
mo - ña pá un to - re - ro. Bue-na ca - pa; buen som-
good life for a to - re - ro. Got a good coat; got a
la la la la la la la la la la la la la la la
mo - ña pá un to - re - ro. Bue-na ca - pa; buen som-
good life for a to - re - ro. Got a good coat; got a
dm d dm dm dm dm dm dm d dm dm

*Omit bracketed notes as required.

30
la la la la la la la la la la la la la la
la la la la la la la la la la la la la la
mf
Yo no sé a-quel-la a - güi - ta lo que te - ní - a,
Down in the Ma - ca - re - na I saw her glanc - ing,
dm dm dm d dm dm dm dm
33
la Ma-ca - re - ni - ta,
la la la la la la la la la la la la la la
la la la la la la la la la la la la la la
yo no sé a-quel-la a - güi - ta lo que te -
down in the Ma - ca - re - na I saw her
dm d d dm dm dm d dm dm

36
la Ma-ca-re-ni - ta,
la la la

43
3
-ni - ta, la,
la la la la la la la la la la la la la la
-bre - ro; bue-na mo - ña pá un to - re - ro. Bue-na
good hat; it's a good life for a to - re - ro. Got a
la la la la la la la la la la la la la la
-bre - ro; bue-na mo - ña pá un to - re - ro. Bue-na
good hat; it's a good life for a to - re - ro. Got a
dm dm d dm dm d dm dm dm dm dm
3

46
la Ma-ca - re - ni - ta. la!
la la la

50
A.
la la! la! la la la la la la la la la la la la la la la la
T.
(solo)
la! la! ch! la la la la la la la la la la la la la la la la
B. 1
La Ma-ca-re - ni - ta,
B. 2
dm dm dm d dm dm dm dm
54
S. 1
la la la la la la la
S. 2
Me la dió u-na mo - ci - ta de fi - li -
Down in the Ma-ca - re - na we live to -
A.
la la la la la la la la la la la la la
T.
la la la la la la la la la la la la la
B. 1
B.2
dm d d dm dm dm d dm dm

57
- gra - na, me la dió u-na mo-
- ge - ther, down in the Ma-ca-
la la la la la la la la la la la la la la
la la la la la la la la la la la la la la
la Ma-ca-re-ni-ta,
dm dm dm d d dm dm

60
la la la la la la la la
-ci - ta de fi - li - gra - na
la más fi-na y pu-
-re - na we live to - ge - ther.
I like the way we're
la la la la la la la la

64
sub. p
la la la la la la la la la
-lí - a de tóa Tri - a - na.
danc - ing through life to - ge - ther.
la la la la la la la la la
sub. p
unis.
la la la la Tri - a - na. La Ma - ca - re - na. Bue - na ca - pa; buen som-
to - ge - ther. The Ma - ca - re - na. Got a good coat; got a
la la la la Tri - a - na.
to - ge - ther.
la la la la la la la la la
la la la Tri - a - na. La Ma - ca - re - na. Bue - na ca - pa; buen som-
to - ge - ther. The Ma - ca - re - na. Got a good coat; got a
dm dm Tri - a - na.
to - ge - ther.
dm dm dm dm d dm dm

68
S.
la la la la la la la la la la la la la la la la la la la la
A.
-bre - ro; bue-na mo - ña pá un to - re - ro. Bue-na ca - pa; buen som-
good hat; it's a good life for a to - re - ro. Got a good coat; got a
T.
la la la la la la la la la la la la la la la la la la la la
B. 1
-bre - ro; bue-na mo - ña pá un to - re - ro. Bue-na ca - pa; buen som-
good hat; it's a good life for a to - re - ro. Got a good coat; got a
B. 2
dm dm d dm dm d dm dm dm dm dm dm d dm dm
72
S. 1
la la la la la la la la la la La
sub. f
S. 2
la la la la la la la la la la la la la la la la la la la la
sub. f
A.
-bre - ro; bue-na mo - ña pá un to - re - ro. Bue-na
good hat; it's a good life for a to - re - ro. Got a
sub. f
T.
la la la la la la la la la la la la la la la la la la la la
sub. f
B. 1
-bre - ro; bue-na mo - ña pá un to - re - ro. Bue-na
good hat; it's a good life for a to - re - ro. Got a
sub. f
B. 2
dm dm d dm dm d dm dm dm dm dm
sub. f

75
la Ma - ca - re - ni - ta,
la la la la la la la la la la la la la
ca - pa; buen som - bre - ro; bue-na mo - ña pá un to -
good coat; got a good hat; it's a good life for a to -
la la la la la la la la la la la la la
ca - pa; buen som - bre - ro; bue-na mo - ña pá un to -
good coat; got a good hat; it's a good life for a to -
dm d dm dm dm dm d dm dm d dm dm

78
la, la Ma - ca - re - ni - ta.
la la la la la la la la la la la la la la
- re - ro. Bue-na ca - pa; buen som - bre - ro; bue-na
- re - ro. Got a good coat; got a good hat; it's a
la la la la la la la la la la la la la la
- re - ro. Bue-na ca - pa; buen som - bre - ro; bue-na
- re - ro. Got a good coat; got a good hat; it's a
dm dm dm dm d dm dm dm dm d dm

81
— to - re - ro. la la!
— la la la pá un to - re - ro.
a to - re - ro. la la!
mo - ña pá un to - re - ro.
good life for a to - re - ro. la la la la la la!
(solo)
— la la la pá un to - re - ro.
a to - re - ro. la la! ch!
mo - ña pá un to - re - ro.
good life for a to - re - ro. la la!
dm d dm pá un to - re - ro.
a to - re - ro. la la!

for Lizzie Maclean

Hush, little baby

Trad. American
arr. BOB CHILCOTT

© Oxford University Press 2008. Photocopying this copyright material is ILLEGAL.

4
p dolce
Hush, lit - tle ba - by, don't say a word,
doo doo doo doo doo doo doo
doo doo do doo doo doo doo doo
dm buh dm dm buh dm buh dm dm buh duh buh
7
Ma-ma's gon-na buy you a mock-in' bird. If that mock - in'
doo doo
doo doo
dm buh dm buh dm dm buh duh buh dm buh dm buh

10
bird don't sing, Ma-ma's gon-na buy you a dia-mond ring. oo
doo doo doo
doo doo doo And
dm dm buh duh buh dm buh dm duh dm dm buh dm

13
oo
oo
if that dia-mond ring turns brass, Ma-ma's gon-na buy you a
dm buh dum buh dm dm buh duh buh dm buh dum buh

16
oo
oo
oo
oo
look-in' glass. If that look - in' glass gets broke,
dm dm buh duh buh dm buh dm buh dm dm buh duh buh

19
mp
And if that bil - ly
mp
And if that bil - ly
mp
Ma-ma's gon - na buy you a bil - ly goat. And if that bil - ly
mp
dm buh dm buh dm dm And if that bil - ly
mp

22
goat won't pull, Ma-ma's gon-na buy you a cart and bull. oo
goat won't pull, Ma-ma's gon-na buy you a cart and bull. oo
goat won't pull, Ma-ma's gon-na buy you a cart and bull. And
goat won't pull, Ma-ma's gon-na buy you a cart and bull. And
25
mf
oo
mf
oo
mf
if that cart and bull turn o - ver, Ma-ma's gon-na buy you a
mf
if that cart and bull turn o - ver, Ma-ma's gon-na buy you a
mf

28
f
And if that dog named Ro - ver don't bark,
And if that dog named Ro - ver don't bark,
dog named Ro - ver. If that dog named Ro - ver don't bark,
dog named Ro - ver. If that dog named Ro - ver don't bark,
poco rit.
31
Ma - ma's gon - na buy you a horse and cart.
Ma - ma's gon - na buy you a horse and cart.
Ma - ma's gon - na buy you a horse and cart.
Ma - ma's gon - na buy you a horse and cart.
poco rit.

33
a tempo
p dolce
If that horse and cart fall down, You'll be the sweet-est lit-tle girl in
p dolce
doo doo doo doo doo lit-tle girl.
p dolce
doo doo doo doo doo lit-tle girl.
p dolce
dm buh dm buh dm dm buh duh buh dm buh dm lit-tle girl.
a tempo
p dolce
37
town.
rit.
pp
oo
doo doo doo doo doo doo doo doo oo
doo doo doo doo doo doo doo doo doo oo
dm buh dm buh dm buh dm dm buh dm buh dm buh dm oo
rit.
pp

for the Japan Choral Association

Sakura
(Cherry tree)

Trad. Japanese
arr. BOB CHILCOTT

English version BC

© Oxford University Press 2008. Photocopying this copyright material is ILLEGAL.

13
mf
S.
A.
sa - ku - ra, sa - ku - ra, ha - na - za - ka - ri.
Cher - ry tree, cher - ry tree, flower - ing far and wide.
T.
B.
mf
mf
17
mp cantabile
21
f espress.
mf dolce
mp
25
poco rit.
a tempo
p

29
p dolce
S.
A.
Sa - ku - ra, sa - ku - ra, ya - yo - i no so - ra wa
Cher - ry tree, cher - ry tree, spreads as far as you can see,
T.
Sa - ku - ra, sa - ku - ra, ya - yo - i no so - ra
Cher - ry tree, cher - ry tree, spreads as far as you can
B.
Sa - ku - ra, sa - ku - ra, ya - yo - i no so - ra wa
Cher - ry tree, cher - ry tree, spreads as far as you can see,
33
cresc.
mf espress.
mi - wa - ta - su ka - gi - ri, ka - su - mi ka ku - mo ka
nes - tled in the arms of spring, in a mist that pas - ses by,
wa mi - wa - ta-su ka - gi - ri, ka - su - mi ka ku - mo ka
see, nes - tled in the arms of spring, in a mist that pas - ses by,
mi - wa - ta - su ka - gi - ri, ka - su - mi ka ku - mo ka
nes - tled in the arms of spring, in a mist that pas - ses by,

37
unis.
mp
S./A.
S.
p
A.
ni - o - i zo i - zu - ru,
fra - grant - ly a - cross the sky.
i - za - ya, i - za - ya,
Come with me, come with me,
T./B.
unis.
mp
T.
B.
p
mp
p
3
41
poco rit.
a tempo
mi - ni - yu - ka - n.
cher - ries blos - som - ing.
poco rit.
a tempo
45
p
rit.
Sa - ku - ra, sa - ku - ra.
Cher - ry tree, cher - ry tree.
p
rit.
pp

for Justin Doyle and the Ryedale Festival

Scarborough Fair

Trad. English
arr. BOB CHILCOTT

© Oxford University Press 2008. Photocopying this copyright material is ILLEGAL.

13
unis.
- mem - ber me to one who lives there,
unis.
f
17
mf
She was once a true love of mine,
S. of
A. of
T.
B.
mf
mf
21
mine.
f
mine, of mine.
unis. mf
Tell her to make me a cam-bric,
unis. mf
f
Tell her to make me a cam - bric
f
mf

25
f
cam - bric shirt. Pars-ley, sage, rose - ma - ry, and
shirt.
f
f
29
thyme. With-out no seam nor fine nee - dle -
33
unis.
mf
-work, Then she'll be a true love of
unis.
mf
mf

37
S.
A.
T.
B.
of mine, of
mine, of mine, of mine, of
41
f
unis.
mine. Ba da ba da ba da ba da da da da da da da da
f
f
44
da ba ba da dp ba da da da da dp ba da da

47
S.
A.
da da da ba da da da da
ba da ba da ba da ba ba
50
da da da da da da ba da ba da ba da da
da dp ba da da da ba da da da ba da da ba da
54
ff
ba dp ba da da da da da da da Oh
T.
B.
da da da da da
ff

57
Scar - bo - rough Fair?
are you going to Scar - bo - rough, Scar - borough Fair? Pars - ley,
ff
61
sage, rose - ma - ry, and thyme. Re -
65
unis.
- mem - ber me to one who lives there,
unis.

69
f
mf
S.
A.
She was once a true love of mine, of
T.
B.
f
mf
f
mf
73
cresc.
mine, of mine,
mine, of mine, of mine, of
cresc.
cresc.
ff
fff
76
mine, of mine.
ff
fff
ff
fff

for Jon Washburn and the Vancouver Chamber Choir

Tell my ma

Children's song from Northern Ireland
arr. BOB CHILCOTT

© Oxford University Press 2008. Photocopying this copyright material is ILLEGAL.

10
my comb, but that's al - right 'til I go home. O
13
she is hand - some, she, she is pret-ty, she is the belle of
16
Bel - fast ci - ty. She is court - in' one, two, three,

19
mf
please won't you tell me, who is she?
Oh, who is she?
mf
mf
22
unis. f
Oh, who is she?
Oh,
unis. f
Al - bert Moon - ey says
25
oh, oh, he says he loves her,
and all the boys are fight-in'
he loves her, all the boys are fight - in' for her,

28
for her. 'Oh, oh, oh, oh are you well?'
knock at the door and ring the bell, 'Oh, my true love, are
31
S.
A.
Oh here she comes as white as snow,
T.
B.
you well?'
34
rings on her fin-gers and bells on her toes. Ol' John-ny Mur-ray, he says

37
she'll die if she does-n't get the fel-low with the ro-vin' eye,
40
mf
the ro-vin' eye,
unis. f
Let the
T.
mf
the ro-vin' eye!
43
wind and the rain and the hail blow high, the snow come tum-bl-in' from
f
Let the wind and the hail blow high,

46
— the sky. She's as nice as ap - ple pie,
snow come tumb - lin'— from the sky. She's as nice as
49
S.
A.
she'll get her own fel-low by— 'n' by. Oh when she gets a lad-
ap - ple, ap-ple pie.
52
— of her own, she won't tell her ma when she— gets home.

55
Let the boys say what they will, it's Al - bert Moon - ey she loves still! Oh
59
ff
tell my ma when I go home, the boys won't leave the girls
ff
Oh tell my ma.
ff
62
a - lone. They pulled my hair and they stole my comb, but
They pulled my hair and they stole my comb,

65
that's al - right 'til I go home. Oh she is hand - some, she,
Oh tell, oh tell my ma.
68
she is pret-ty, she is the belle of Bel - fast ci - ty.
71
She is court - in' one, two, three, please won't you tell me,

74
who is she? Oh she is hand - some, she, she is pret-ty,
77
she is the belle of Bel - fast ci - ty. She is court - in' one,
80
two, three, please won't you tell me, who is she?

for Waverley Care and its work supporting those in Scotland whose lives are touched by HIV

The House of the Rising Sun

Trad. American
arr. BOB CHILCOTT

© Oxford University Press 2008. Photocopying this copyright material is ILLEGAL.

9
been the ru - in of ma - ny a poor girl, And
12
dim.
mp
me, O God, for one.
dim.
mp
unis. mp
Go
dim.
mp
15
cresc.
T./B.
tell my ba - by sis - ter,
T.
B.
f
Ne - ver do like I have
cresc.
f

18
done, Tell her to shun that house in New Or - leans,
21
mf
They call the Ris - ing Sun.
mf
24
S.
A.
mf
If I'd-a list-ened what my ma - ma said, I'd-a
T.
B.
mf

27
f
been at home to - day, Be - ing so young and
f
f
30
ff
fool - ish, poor boy, Let a ram - bler lead me a -
ff
ff
33
- stray.
mf

36
S.
A.
T.
B.
p
One foot is on the
p
p
38
plat - form, The o - ther one on the train, I'm
41
mp
go - in' back to New Or - leans To
mp
mp

44
p
wear that ball and chain.
p
p
47
SOPRANO SOLO p
Go - in' back to
p
A.
oo
T.
B.
p
50
New Or - leans, My race is al - most run,
oo

TUTTI
53
mp
S.
A.
Go - in'_ to spend_ the rest of my life,_ Be -
T.
B.
mp
mp
56
- neath_ the Ris - ing Sun,_ be - neath_ the Ris - ing
59
p
rit.
Sun,_ be - neath_ the Ris - ing Sun.
p
rit.
p

Tuoll′ on mun kultani

(There is my loved one)

Trad. Finnish
arr. BOB CHILCOTT

English version BC

© Oxford University Press 2008. Photocopying this copyright material is ILLEGAL.

7
Voi mi-nun kul - ta-ni, voi mi-nun lin - tu-ni, kun et tu-le jo,
Ah you, my loved one, ah you, my dear one, still you do not come,

kun et tu - le jo!
still you do not come!
10
kun et tu - le jo!
still you do not come!
mm
kun et tu - le jo!
still you do not come!
mm

13
p
oo
mp più espress.
Lin - nut ne lau - la-vat so - ri - al - la suul - la, so - ri - am - pi kul - ta - ni
Hear - ing the song of the birds high a - bove me Fills me with the hope that you

16
oo
oo
unis.
ää - ni on kuul - la. Voi mi-nun kul - ta-ni, voi mi-nun lin - tu-ni,
real - ly could love me. Ah you, my loved one, ah you, my dear one,

*If the repeat is made the choir should re-enter at bar 23.

25
ah
ah
ah
ah
ah
ah
3
28
mf
mp
3
ah
ah
mf
mp
ah
ah
mf
mp
ah
ah
mf
mp
ah
ah
3
3
mf
mp

31
pp
Tu-le, tu-le kul-ta-ni,
Come to me, my loved one,
mm
34
S.
A.
T.
B.
tu-le ko-ti puo-leen, taik-ka jo me-neh-dyn-kin i-kä-vään ja huo-leen.
come and be be-side me Or I'll sure-ly die of the love I hold in-side me.
37
Voi mi-nun kul-ta-ni, voi mi-nun lin-tu-ni, kun et tu-le jo,
Ah you, my loved one, ah you, my dear one, still you do not come,

40
kun et tu - le jo,
still you do not come,
kun et tu - le
still you do not
kun et tu - le jo,
still you do not come,
mm
kun et tu - le jo,
still you do not come,
mm
mm
pp
43
jo,
come,
molto rit.
slower
ppp
unis.
mm
kun et tu-le jo!
still you do not come!
unis.
ppp
molto rit.
slower
8
ppp

for Justin Doyle and the Dorking Choral Society

Waltzing Matilda

A. B. 'Banjo' Paterson (1864–1941)

Trad. Australian
arr. BOB CHILCOTT

Text and melody reproduced by permission of Carl Fischer LLC for North America.
Music © Oxford University Press 2008. Photocopying this copyright material is ILLEGAL.

16
bil - ly boiled, 'Who'll come a - waltz - ing Ma - til - da with
21
f
Waltz - ing Ma - til - da, waltz - ing Ma-
me?
f
f
25
- til - da, who'll come a - waltz - ing Ma - til - da with me?'
And he

30
mf
S.
A.
oo
mf
T.
oo
mf
B.
sang as he sat and wait-ed till his bil-ly boiled,
mf

35
f
S.
A.
'Who'll come a-waltz-ing Ma - til - - da with me?'
T.
B.
f
f
f

41
unis.
mf
A - long came a jum - buck to drink at the
unis.
mf
A - long came a jum - buck
mf
46
bil - la - bong, Up jumped the swag - man and grabbed him with
T.
B.
to drink and he grabbed,
50
glee, And he sang as he shoved that jum-buck in his
grabbed him with glee, And he sang,

54
S.
A.
tuck-er - bag, 'You'll come a - waltz-ing Ma - til - da with
sang,
59
f
me. Waltz - ing Ma - til - da, waltz - ing Ma-
f
f
63
- til - da, you'll come a - waltz-ing Ma - til - da with me.'
And he

68
mf
oo
mf
oo
mf
sang as he shoved that jum-buck in his tuck-er - bag,
mf

73
f
'You'll come a-waltz-ing Ma - til - - da with me.'
f
f

*If the repeat is made the choir should re-enter at bar 60.

93
Oh, You'll come a - waltz - ing Ma - til - da with
97
me. Waltz - ing Ma - til - da, waltz - ing Ma-
101
- til - da, you'll come a - waltz-ing Ma - til - da with me.'

106
mf
S.
A.
oo
mf
T.
oo
mf
B.
Who's that jol - ly jum - buck you've got in your tuck-er - bag,
mf

111
f
S.
A.
'Who'll come a-waltz-ing Ma - til - - da with me?'
T.
B.
f
f

117
unis.
Up jumped the swag - man, leapt in - to the
unis.
122
sub. p
bil - la - bong, 'You'll ne - ver catch me a - live,' said he, And his
sub. p
sub. p
127
ghost may be heard as you pass by the bil - la - bong,

131
S.
A.
oo
Oh,
T.
oo
Oh,
B.
'Who'll come a - waltz - ing Ma - til - da with me? Oh,

136
p cresc.
S.
A.
Waltz - ing Ma - til - da, waltz - ing Ma - til - da,
T.
B.
p cresc.
p cresc.

140
you'll come a - waltz - ing Ma - til - da with me.'
And his
mp
144
mp
oo
mp
oo
ghost may be heard as you pass by the bil - la - bong,
mp

149
mf cresc.
S.
A.
'Who'll come_ a - waltz - ing Ma - til - da with me? Oh,_
T.
B.
mf cresc.
mf cresc.
153
ff
Waltz - ing_ Ma - til - da, waltz - ing_ Ma - til - da,
ff
ff
157
you'll come_ a - waltz - ing Ma - til - da with me.'
And_ his

161
mf
oo
mf
oo
mf
ghost may be heard as you pass by the bil-la - bong,
mf
166
'Who'll come a - waltz - ing Ma - til - - - da with
170
mp
unis.
p
me?'
Waltz - ing Ma - til - da.
unis.
mp
p
mp
p

CD track list and credits

The CD included with the spiral-bound edition of *Jazz Folk Songs for Choirs* (ISBN 978-0-19-336182-9) contains jazz-trio backings for the seven accompanied songs in the collection and a pronunciation guide for each of the foreign-language texts.

Track list

Jazz-trio backings:

1. À la claire fontaine
2. Sakura
3. Scarborough Fair
4. Tell my ma
5. The House of the Rising Sun
6. Tuoll' on mun kultani
7. Waltzing Matilda

Foreign-language poems:

8. À la claire fontaine (French)
9. La Macarenita (Spanish)
10. Sakura (Japanese)
11. Tuoll' on mun kultani (Finnish)

CD credits

Piano: Alexander Hawkins
Bass: Michael Chilcott
Drums: Derek Scurll

French speaker: Agnès Ausseur
Spanish speaker: Karen Fodor
Japanese speaker: Hidemi Hatada
Finnish speaker: Silja Murto

Recorded on 29 April 2008 at the Royal College of Music Studios, London, by Stephen Harrington. Mastered by Tim Turan at Turan Audio.